IRISH TRACTION
in Colour

IRISH TRACTION
in Colour

Derek Huntriss

Ian Allan
PUBLISHING

Acknowledgments:

I would like to take this opportunity to thank the following people for their generous contribution of time and knowledge in the preparation and checking of this title.

A heartfelt thankyou goes to John Langford, a retired Traincrew Manager on British Railways, for his massive contribution in preparing and checking the manuscript. To John Edgington, former member of the library staff at The National Railway Museum, for sharing his in-depth knowledge of Irish railway history with additional anecdotal information in the captioning of the pictures used and for reading and checking the final page proofs. Finally to Neville Simms of Coventry, a lifelong friend and RCTS member for checking the manuscript and those of many previous efforts.

As always deepest thanks are offered to all the photographers whose work is included in these pages. Without their efforts in recording the railway scene over up to 50 years ago this title could not have been contemplated.

Bibliography:

Jeremy Clements / Michael McMahon: *Locomotives of the GSR;* Colourpoint

Tom Ferris: *The Great Northern Railway — An Irish Railway Pictorial;* Midland Publishing

Tom Ferris: *The Irish Narrow Gauge — A Pictorial History — Vol 1 From Cork to Cavan;* The Blackstaff Press

Patrick J. Flanagan: *The Cavan & Leitrim Railway;* David & Charles

Irish Railway Record Society: *Irish Railways in Pictures — No 1 The Great Northern*

Irish Railway Record Society: *Irish Railways in Pictures — No 2 The Midland Great Western Line*

Irish Railway Record Society: *Irish Railways in Pictures — No 3 The Railways of Cork*

Irish Railway Record Society: *Irish Railways in Pictures — No 4 The Giant's Causeway Tramway*

Norman Johnston: *The Irish Narrow Gauge in Colour;* Colourpoint

Padraig O'Cuimin: *The Baronial Lines of the MGWR — Loughrea & Ballinrobe;* Transport Research Associates

Robert Robotham / Joe Curran: *The Wee Donegal Revisited;* Colourpoint

David G. Rowlands: *The Tralee & Dingle Railway;* Bradford Barton

W. Ernest Shepherd: *The Dublin & South Eastern Railway;* David & Charles

Ernie Shepherd: *Cork, Bandon & South Coast Railway;* Midland Publishing

Neil Sprinks: *Sligo, Leitrim & Northern Counties Railway;* Midland Publishing

Stephen Johnson: *Johnson's Atlas & Gazetteer of the Railways of Ireland;* Midland Publishing

Other Publications: *Backtrack, Modern Railways, Railway Magazine, Railway World, Steam Days, Trains Illustrated, History of Railways, Great Trains, The World of Trains, RCTS Railway Observer.*

Derek Huntriss
Coventry
January 2011

Front cover: **UTA Class Vs 4-4-0 No 207 *Boyne* passes Portadown with an excursion for Dublin on 1 September 1964. Having received a general overhaul at Dundalk before being returned by CIE to the UTA in June 1963, No 207 remained Belfast Adelaide shed's main line express engine before being withdrawn for cutting up in 1965.** *Alan Jarvis*

Back cover, top: **Having received a fresh coat of paint on a recent visit to Inchicore Works ex-Tralee & Dingle 2-6-0T No 6T awaits departure from Ballinamore with the daily train over the branch, the 1.50pm to Arigna, on 26 May 1958. The daily train was run as a mixed as required and took 1hr 25min for the journey, returning from Arigna at 4.15pm.** *J. Edgington*

Back cover, bottom: **CIE 'A' class Co-Co diesel No A11 enters Killiney & Ballybrack with a down train from Dublin in May 1959. The £4¾ million contract for Metropolitan-Vickers Electrical Co Ltd to supply 94 diesel-electric locomotives to CIE was at that time the biggest contract ever placed in Britain for diesel locomotives.** *Colour-Rail*

Half-title page: **A timeless scene captured in October 1962 as ex-MGWR Class J19 0-6-0 No 610 awaits its next turn of duty outside the shed at Ballaghaderreen. At that time the branch service from Kilfree Junction consisted of a twice-daily 'mixed train' in each direction.** *Roy Hobbs*

Title page: **The crew of CDRJC Class 5 2-6-4T No 4 *Meenglas* pose for the camera in late evening light at Donegal in May 1959. Rolling stock and other items were purchased by an American, Dr Cox, soon after closure at the end of 1959. The high cost of shipment, estimated at £35,000, prevented the material crossing the Atlantic.** *Derek Penney*

First published 2011

ISBN 978 0 7110 3459 4

All rights reserved. No part of this book may be reproduced or transmitted in any form or by any means, electronic or mechanical, including photocopying, recording, scanning or by any information storage and retrieval system, on the internet or elsewhere, without permission from the Publisher in writing.

© Ian Allan Publishing Ltd 2011

Published by Ian Allan Publishing

an imprint of Ian Allan Publishing Ltd, Hersham, Surrey KT12 4RG.
Printed in England by Ian Allan Printing Ltd, Hersham, Surrey KT12 4RG.

Visit the Ian Allan Publishing website at www.ianallanpublishing.com

Distributed in the Unites States of America and Canada by BookMasters Distribution Services.

Code 1104/B

Contents

Introduction 6

Northern Counties Committee 12

Narrow- gauge 24

Sligo, Leitrim & Northern Counties 36

Great Northern 40

Midland Great Western 62

Great Southern & Western 74

Dublin & South Eastern 88

Cork, Bandon & South Coast 92

Introduction

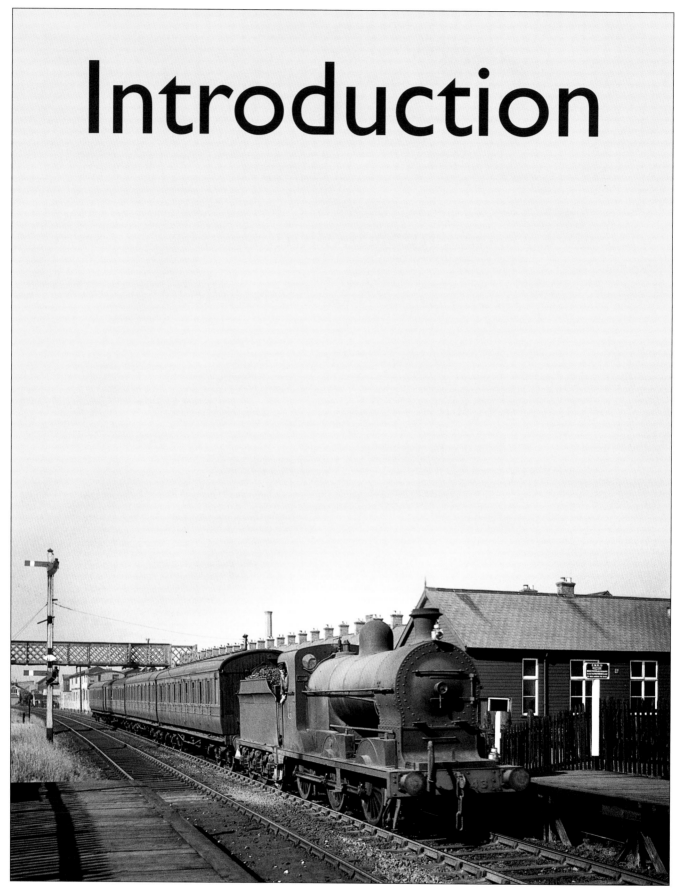

The driver smiles for the photographer in this classic GNR (I) picture as GN Class SG 0-6-0 No 43 arrives at Adelaide at the head of a rake of teak-liveried stock in May 1959. With the introduction of the 'SG' class in 1913 the standard driving wheel for goods engines was increased from 4ft 7¼in to 5ft 1in diameter. In 1921 the enlarged version of the 'SG' class was introduced as Class SG3 with larger cylinders and boiler. *Derek Penney*

The history of Irish railways is a diverse and complex story born out of social, political and economic change. Within the limits of this title it is obviously impossible to cover every aspect of so large a subject, the reader being recommended to undertake further study from the many excellent titles available, particularly those listed in the bibliography. The pictorial content is based on the available material from many well known and less known photographers, with a conscious effort to present mainly unpublished pictures and is representative of the 1950s/1960s when the last steam locomotives were still in operation alongside the newer diesel locomotives and units that were to replace them. After the end of World War 2 radical alterations took place both north and south of the border in motive power, rolling stock and even the structure of the Irish railway system.

By the early 1960s 'dieselisation' of regular scheduled services was virtually complete and had been achieved gradually since 1952, when the first of the AEC railcar sets was delivered. These cars were the salvation of the CIE network as they provided fast, economical services with a degree of comfort which did much to retrieve the flagging passenger traffic. The travelling public associated these railcars with a rejuvenation of the lines they served and as a result there was public approval for the bold step taken in 1954 when an order for 94 diesel locomotives was placed with Metropolitan-Vickers of Manchester. With this and subsequent orders, there was enough motive power to supplant the ageing stock of steam locomotives then in use.

North of the border the former Great Northern Railway Board — successor to the GNR (I) — was dissolved as from 30 September 1958. The portion of the undertaking in Northern Ireland was amalgamated with the UTA while the remainder in the Republic was taken over by CIE. The locomotives and rolling stock of the GNR were divided evenly between the two undertakings. Thus divided the GNR was only a shadow of its former self. It comprised the lines from Dublin to Belfast with the Howth, Oldcastle, Ardee, 'Irish North', Warrenpoint and Antrim branches, and

from Portadown to Derry, with a branch from Cookstown, by then goods only, this closing in 1959 except for the section to Coalisland. The 'Irish North', which except for freight closed in October 1957, lost even that breath of life from 1 January 1960.

The UTA itself had not stood still. It had completely dieselised its Belfast–Bangor section in 1953 with 28 multi-engined, multiple-unit railcars and from 1958 a similar position was achieved on the NCC Belfast–Coleraine–Derry line. Whereas the CIE employed diesel locomotives, the UTA placed its faith in diesel railcars, many of which were converted from existing passenger coaches. Following World War 2, the UTA had relentlessly removed branch lines until the only lines of the former NCC system to remain were those from Belfast to Derry, with the branch from Coleraine to Portrush and the 'Shore Road' from Bleach Green Junction to Larne Harbour. The last of the branches to go was the Cookstown Junction–Kilrea section of the erstwhile Derry Central line which had lost its passenger traffic at the end of August 1950 and which closed completely from 1 October 1959.

The three narrow-gauge lines which survived until 1959-61 lasted long enough to attract a good number of photographers and are illustrated here. These were the Cavan & Leitrim and West Clare sections of CIE and the ever popular County Donegal.

At various times over the last 30 years the railway systems north and south of the border have been threatened with extinction. Today they are worked by two companies — Irish Rail and Northern Ireland Railways. Despite a low population density away from the main cities, a reasonable network of lines is operated, and considerable investment is continuing, particularly in the Belfast and Dublin areas.

While rail developments in Ireland may seem modest in comparison to some EC countries, they are important in confirming recognition by the Governments involved that railways have a vital role to play in the 21st century, something that was unclear in the 1970s/1980s.

Below: The scene at Ballysodare is captured in this picture taken on 7 May 1957 as Sligo, Leitrim & Northern Counties Railway 0-6-4T *Lough Erne* shunts its train. The SLNCR ran into the MGWR at Carrignagat Junction, one mile south of the station. However the GSR took out the junction and the SLNCR and MGWR routes ran as single lines to Ballysodare which then became the actual junction. *T. B. Owen*

Bottom: The driver of CDRJC 2-6-4T No 4 *Meenglas* nonchalantly reads the newspaper as his train awaits Customs clearance at Castlefin in May 1959 — a Customs official can be seen above the first wagon in the train on the opposite platform. The trestle table for Customs inspections can be seen in the shed, normal operations being to carry out procedures in the open. *Derek Penney*

Top: **UTA 'U' class 4-4-0 No 66 *Meath* (ex-GN No 201) is posed for the camera at Belfast Adelaide shed in May 1959. Five earlier members of this class of light 4-4-0 were constructed in 1915, No 66 surviving until 1965.** *Derek Penney*

Above: **NCC 2-6-0 Mogul No 97 *Earl of Ulster* is depicted outside Belfast York Road shed on 9 May 1957. Constructed in 1936, No 97 took its name from one of the titles of the Duke of Gloucester who was visiting the province at that time.** *T. B. Owen*

No apologies are made for including this previously published picture of GN
Class Vs 4-4-0 No 207 *Boyne* as it waits to take a Belfast express away from
Dublin Amiens Street on 7 May 1959. The division of the GNR in 1958 meant
that Nos 206/7/9 were then allocated to CIE. *T. B. Owen*

Above: **UTA/NIR DMU No 49 is the 15.05 from Larne as it passes sister unit No 53 outside Belfast York Road shed on 15 June 1965. Both units are non-corridor multiple-purpose Brake Seconds.** *Derrick Codling*

Below: **CIE 'B' class diesel No B108 is seen inside Inchicore Works in May 1964. When new, the Class B diesels carried a striking livery of silver — which did not wear well. However, less than one year later some locomotives were repainted in black.** *Colour-Rail*

Northern Counties Committee

NCC 'U2' 'Castle' class 4-4-0 No 74 *Dunluce Castle* stands at Belfast York Road shed on 10 June 1961. The 'U2s' eventually totalled 18 in number and most bore names of castles in Ulster. Seven of these locomotives had been built by North British in Glasgow, hence the enginemen's title 'Scotchmen'. Today this locomotive is preserved in crimson livery at the Ulster Folk & Transport Museum at Cultra. *T. B. Owen*

Serving the north-east of Ireland, the Northern Counties Committee (NCC) was constructed to the Irish standard gauge of 5ft 3in, a number of 3ft 0in narrow gauge lines being acquired later. It had its origins in the Belfast & Ballymena Railway which had opened to traffic on 11 April 1848, although the NCC itself came into existence on 1 July 1903 as a result of the Midland Railway taking over the Belfast & Northern Counties Railway (BNCR). At the 1923 Grouping of British railway companies, the Committee became part of the LMS railway and passed to the British Transport Commission upon the nationalisation of the railways in Britain in 1948. In the following year, 1949, it was sold to the Ulster Transport Authority (UTA).

The BNCR had recognised the potential value of tourism and had influenced its development throughout the north of Ireland. In addition it was able to exploit the advantages of the short sea route between Stranraer and Larne which gained strategic importance during World War 2. The BNCR continued the B&BR's practice of running cheap excursions. In addition to those promoted by the company itself, there were extensive summer programmes of special trains operated on behalf of outside organisations, especially Sunday schools and other church bodies. As well as these there were a large number of special trains chartered by Loyalist organisations around the 'Twelfth of July' and the 'Twelfth of August'.

The Giant's Causeway became an even greater tourist attraction in 1887 with the opening of the Giant's Causeway & Bush Valley Electric Tramway. An attraction in itself, thousands of tourists found the journey from outside Portrush railway station much quicker and easier than before on what was the world's first hydro-electric tramway.

Early locomotives of the constituent companies were constructed to assorted designs from a number of manufacturers, the first locomotives for the Belfast & Ballymena Railway being purchased from Bury, Curtis and Kennedy. These were four 2-2-2 Singles and one 0-4-2 goods locomotive. At a later date four more 2-2-2s were ordered, but this time from Sharp Bros.

MR (NCC) locomotive policy continued BNCR practice and was largely independent of Derby until Bowman Malcolm retired at the end of 1922. Midland Railway and LMS influence became increasingly apparent during the building and renewal programmes carried out by Malcolm's successors, W. K. Wallace and, at a later date, H. P. Stewart. The delivery of three standard G7 boilers from Derby in 1923 began the standardisation and modernisation of NCC locomotives. Two of these were used for the rebuilding of 'Light Compounds' Nos 59 and 62 into Class U1 4-4-0 locomotives. With few exceptions from this time on, Derby works could deal more economically with boilers than York Road. These would be returned some four or five months later with a new firebox fitted ready for installation in the next suitable locomotive due to come into the works.

As with the locomotives, the Midland Railway influence on NCC coaching stock became apparent following the retirement of Bowman Malcolm. Being a small railway the NCC did not require the variety of vehicles needed by the parent LMS. However, the NCC did provide for three classes of passenger accommodation, resulting in several designs that were unique to the NCC. The LMS (NCC) coaching stock largely conformed to LMS Period 1 designs. Mounted on steel under-frames that were generally 57ft long and weighing between 28 and 31 tons, they continued to be constructed into the 1930s as repeat orders. Side-corridor stock such as the J6 Thirds and F2 Composites had doors with adjacent quarter lights and ventilation was by droplights set into the doors.

Today, the former NCC main line from Belfast to Londonderry, the Larne line and the branch to Portrush remain open and are operated by Northern Ireland Railways.

A number of NCC railway items have survived into the preservation era and include Class U2 4-4-0 No 74 *Dunluce Castle* which is on display at the Ulster Folk and Transport Museum at Cultra. Another locomotive, which has seen regular use on excursions, is Class WT 2-6-4T No 4, which is owned and operated by the Railway Preservation Society of Ireland.

Right: **NCC 2-6-4T No 52 is depicted with a goods train at Londonderry Waterside on 1 September 1964. With plans for a new road immediately adjacent to the old station at Londonderry Waterside and extensive bomb damage, a new station was opened by NIR on 24 February 1980.** *Alan Jarvis*

Above: **This picture taken in November 1969 shows NIR railcar No 63 against the buffer stops at Portrush station. No 63, a multi-purpose (passenger & goods) DMU, emerged from the Duncrue Street Works in November 1961. This and car No 64 differed from existing cars in that they had driving cabs in a left-hand driving position at each end of the car. They could then operate as single units if required, unlike the previous cars which had right-hand drive and had to run in pairs.**
H. Luff / Online Transport Archive

Left: **NCC 2-6-4T No 10 heads away from Portrush with a return excursion to Belfast on 14 July 1964. Following the success of the NCC Moguls it is not surprising that the new 2-6-4Ts were merely a tank engine version of the 2-6-0, which itself had been more based on the Fowler 2-6-4T than any LMS Mogul.** *Neville Simms*

Above: **Another view at Portrush, this time depicting UTA 2-6-4Ts Nos 51, 53 and 4 as they await departure with a special additional passenger working to Belfast York Road on Saturday 31 May 1969. Locomotives went up to Coleraine for turning and servicing between morning and evening trains and on this day many took Sunday school children for a day out at the seaside.**

Below: **UTA 2-6-4Ts Nos 5 and 52 await departure from Portrush on 14 July 1964 with the 19.20 and 19.35 departures to Belfast. No 5 was in the first batch of four supplied, entering service on 8 August 1946. With the arrival of the second batch (Nos 1-4 and 9-10) in May and June 1947, five of Larne shed's allocation of seven 4-4-0s were replaced by four of the new tanks, Nos 2-5.** *Derrick Codling (both)*

Above: **UTA 2-6-4T No 53 has arrived at Ballymena with a special additional passenger working on 31 May 1969. By 1964 the NCC 2-6-4 tanks were the only class of steam locomotive in Ireland still intact and numerically they constituted the largest class of passenger locomotive ever built for an Irish railway.** *Derrick Codling*

Below: **Un-named NCC 'Castle'/'U2' class 4-4-0 No 85 is portrayed at Ballymena on 9 May 1957. Prior to the 1940s the platform behind the locomotive was used by the narrow-gauge Ballymena, Cushendall & Red Bay and the Ballymena & Larne Railways.** *T. B. Owen*

Top: **UTA 2-6-4T No 7 is seen at Larne on Friday 12 July 1963 shunting the stock of the 5.15pm 'Orangemen's' special from Ballyclare Junction. This special had arrived at Larne after traversing the Monkstown–Greenisland 'Back Line'.** *John Langford*

Above: **A general view of Larne station taken on 3 September 1964 as UTA 2-6-4T No 3 shunts the yard. The station depicted here closed in 1974 and was replaced by a new station called Larne Town which is situated ¼ mile further round the bay.** *Alan Jarvis*

Right: **UTA 2-6-4T No 7 awaits departure from Larne Harbour on 22 August 1963. No 7 was possibly the most travelled 2-6-4T of them all, having a long spell on the BCDR and later at Adelaide. During the 1954/5 winter, when the Tolka bridge in Dublin was out of action, both Nos 4 and 7 were transferred to the Dublin area for main-line work as the turntable at the Dublin end was cut off.** *Neville Fields*

Above: **Bunker-first UTA 2-6-4T No 9 passes the tablet catcher at Ballycarry with a special passenger working from Larne Harbour to Belfast on 13 July 1964. Following the delivery of Nos 9/10 in May / June 1947 much of the NCC locomotive distribution was drastically overhauled. On the regular interval timetable the locomotive arriving at Larne at about 10min to the hour could return almost immediately at the even hour by quickly running round its train.** *Derrick Codling*

Left: **A pair of UTA 'Jeep' 2-6-4Ts top and tail a loaded spoil train away from Whitehead in May 1969. Three sets of 20 wagons were in use each day with four locomotives. A new motorway (the M2) was being built to link Belfast with the towns in the north of Ulster. The 4,500,000 tons of earth required for the project were obtained as waste from the quarry at Magheramorne Cement Works near Larne and was transported from there by rail to Fortwilliam on the Belfast foreshore.** *Rob Vallance*

Top: **UTA 2-6-4T No 10 is featured again as it heads a northbound passenger train away from Whitehead on 13 July 1964. Like No 9, No 10 was always noted as an excellent running engine. Early in 1948 it was tested on the Bangor line and eventually had another spell in service on those workings and in fact it was one of the last locomotives to work commuter traffic to Bangor before complete dieselisation.** *Neville Simms*

Above: **Another picture featuring No 10 at Whitehead, this time with a special from Larne Harbour to Belfast, also on 13 July 1964.** *Derrick Codling*

Right: **A May 1969 picture of a UTA 2-6-4T locomotive at the head of a spoil train being filled by a tipper lorry at Magheramorne. Between 14 November 1966 and 2 May 1970, when the project was completed, some 7,600 steam-hauled trains of Northern Irish Railways had carried more than 4,000,000 tons of quarry spoil.** *Rob Vallance*

Above: **Ex-SLNCR No 27** *Lough Erne* **is seen outside Belfast York Road shed on 24 August 1963. Following the closure of the SLNCR on 30 September 1957 this and sister locomotive** *Lough Melvin* **were stored in the ex-GNR (I) shed at Enniskillen and were auctioned to the UTA for £700 each at a sale in Belfast on 16 December 1959.** *Neville Fields*

Below: **UTA 2-6-0 No 94** *The Maine* **is seen undergoing repair in this view taken inside York Road Works on 10 May 1957. The parts for locomotives Nos 94/5 were fabricated at Derby Works and shipped over for assembly at York Road, the cost of each locomotive being recorded as £5,507, noticeably cheaper than Nos 90-3.** *T. B. Owen*

Above: **This detailed portrait of UTA 2-6-4T No 51 was taken outside York Road shed on 10 May 1957. The late driver Meneely of Larne had a passion for No 51 and could often be seen after a run polishing away at the numberplate as a preliminary to the latest story of her prowess against the despised rival No 1.**

Below: **One of two LMS 'Jinty' 0-6-0Ts transferred to the NCC in 1944 and used for shunting in the York Road yards, UTA Class Y No 19 is engaged on shunting duties near York Road on 10 June 1961. No 19 was built by Hunslet in 1928, becoming LMS No 16636, being later renumbered 7553.** *T. B. Owen (both)*

Left: Seen outside Belfast York Road shed on 13 July 1964, UTA 0-4-0 diesel No 16 was built by Harland & Wolff in 1937 for internal use as a works shunter. It was transferred to the UTA in 1957 and survived in operation until withdrawal in 1967. *Derrick Codling*

Left: Built at Derby in 1923, Ex- NCC Class V 0-6-0 No 13X (formerly 13) is captured on shunting duties near Belfast York Road in July 1962, the X denoting that it was confined to shunting duties and not allowed on the main line. *J. Carter*

Below: UTA Brake Composite Open unit No 28 is depicted outside Belfast York Road shed on 15 June 1965. This multi-purpose unit was built in 1952 and remained in traffic with NIR until 1978. *Derrick Codling*

Above: **Ex-SLNCR 0-6-4T No 27** *Lough Erne* **is depicted in the docks operated by Belfast Harbour Commissioners on 24 March 1964.** *Lough Erne* **and** *Lough Melvin* **were delivered new to the SLNCR in July 1951 though remaining Beyer-Peacock property. A peculiarity of the SLNCR was that its locomotives were never numbered and were known solely by their names.**

Below: **Another picture of an ex-SLNCR 0-6-4T, this time No 26** *Lough Melvin* **shunting across a street near the docks on 18 May 1964. These two SLNCR 0-6-4Ts had larger cylinders than their predecessors and also had under-slung instead of over-hung coupled wheel springing, improving their stability.** *M. Collins (both)*

Narrow-gauge

CDRJC No 6 *Columbkille* is depicted at Strabane in May 1959. The name *Columbkille* comes from St Columbkille, Scotland's most revered saint, who, in Ireland, is honoured second only to St Patrick. St Columbkille was born of royal bloodlines in Northern Ireland in December 521 and is credited with taking Christianity to Scotland. No 6 was built in 1907 as No 18 *Killybegs*, becoming *Columbkille* in 1937. *Derek Penney*

The narrow-gauge railways in Ireland stood out from other systems in the British Isles. Firstly there were over 550 miles of public railway, more than twice that of the combined total of those in England, Scotland and Wales. In contrast to the lines operated in Wales, Scotland and England, where there are at least 10 different gauges, those in Ireland were built to a 'standard' gauge of 3ft 0in as were the two main systems on the Isle of Man.

Another feature of the narrow-gauge lines which operated in Ireland was that they were all built as common carriers and accepted passengers, parcels, mails, goods, livestock and minerals, almost anything that needed transporting. To a large extent many of them were built in the poorest parts of the country which were particularly the mountainous areas in the west. This however cannot be said of the Cavan & Leitrim Railway which was in one part a roadside tramway.

Following the opening of the Co Antrim narrow-gauge lines in the 1870s the number of new lines grew rapidly. These fell into two distinct types of operation — a few urban but mostly rural roadside tramways and the second being built using their own formation with occasional roadside sections.

With the opening of the Tralee & Dingle in 1891, the narrow-gauge lines began to appear in the more hilly districts. Together with the opening of County Donegal lines to Killybegs (1893) and Glenties (1895) these lines were built with Government assistance under the Light Railways (Ireland) Act. With growing traffic on these and other lines, more powerful locomotives were constructed, particularly 2-6-0Ts, 2-6-2Ts, 4-6-0Ts and 4-6-2Ts.

The final developments to the Irish narrow-gauge network were made in the early 1900s, but the development of motorised road transport between the wars put many lines under threat. The most vulnerable were the roadside tramways, although the Dublin & Lucan saved itself by electrifying in 1900. Closures began with the Listowel & Ballybunion Mono-rail in 1924, closely followed by the Portstewart Tramway in 1926. The UK railway strike in 1933 led to the demise of the Castlederg & Victoria Bridge and most of the NCC narrow-gauge lines with the exception of the Ballycastle line. The next to succumb was the Cork, Blackrock & Passage in 1932, the Cork & Muskerry in 1934 and in 1935 the LLSR began to retract, switching to road services over the next 10 years.

The County Donegal fought back by introducing railcars for its passenger services, as did the Clogher Valley Railway. Hostilities in World War 2 led to the demise of the LLSR's Burtonport extension in 1940 with the closure of the Clogher Valley Railway at the end of 1941. After the war a number of run-down lines gave up the ghost and closed and in the Irish Free State the fuel emergencies of 1947 led to the closures of most narrow-gauge lines, although many reopened after a few months.

The pictures shown here are largely representative of the lines that survived into the late 1950s. In an effort to present mainly unpublished material some lines have been omitted where the images would repeat those seen in other well known colour titles on this subject. We are very fortunate that those lines remaining in the late 1950s attracted the attention of a good number of photographers, some anonymous and some well known, who recorded long-gone scenes for us to enjoy some 50 years later.

As in Scotland and England, preservation of narrow-gauge railways in Ireland has been much less fortunate than Wales. Most of its narrow-gauge network disappeared in the late 1950s and early 1960s, the last public line, the West Clare, closing early in 1961. However, the narrow-gauge railways in Ireland never completely disappeared with the continued operation of the Bord na Mona peat bog railways, albeit with diesel traction.

Although no Irish lines were preserved at the time of closure it is fortunate that a reasonable amount of rolling stock has survived. Today there are representatives of the County Donegal Railway, Cavan & Leitrim, Tralee & Dingle and West Clare railways, all operating to some degree in the hands of enthusiasts, three of them with steam traction and others hoping to join their ranks.

Left: Totally oblivious to the approach of former C&L No 3L with a mixed train on the tramway section of the Cavan & Leitrim Railway's Arigna branch near Ballinamore, these two smiling gentlemen pedalling along on their track bicycle are in for a rude awakening. All highly dangerous in today's world, but Ireland in 1957 was a much different place, with very few cars. *T. B. Owen*

Left: Seconds later, when No 3L came into view, they had to quickly manhandle their machine across the road out of the way next to the photographer's motor cycle. These pictures were taken on 4 June 1957. *T. B. Owen*

Below: In this view taken on 6 May 1957 looking east towards Belturbet from the footbridge at Ballinamore we see a locomotive coming off shed and a coal train which has arrived from Arigna. In the bottom right of the picture is the up platform shelter which had previously been used as a refreshment room. The platform for the Arigna branch is clearly signed indicating 'change for Drumshambo branch'. *T. B. Owen*

Above: **Ex-Tralee & Dingle Kerr-Stuart No 4T is seen outside the shed at Ballinamore on 6 May 1957. By the late 1950s an air of decay pervaded the Cavan & Leitrim section which had become a dumping ground for locomotives with peeling paint, dilapidated carriages and other cast-offs from other closed narrow-gauge railways.** *T. B. Owen*

Below: **With the engine shed on the right, ex-T&D Hunslet 2-6-0T No 3T waits for departure from Ballinamore with the daily 1.50pm to Arigna. The line was worked on the electric staff system.** *T. B. Owen*

Above: **A charming picture of rural Ireland as a coal train from Derreenavoggy crosses the road on the approach to Arigna station. These trains were generally made up of 10 wagons, the coal often destined for the cement works at Drogheda via Belturbet or that at Limerick via Dromod.** *J. Edgington*

Below: **A busy scene at Drumshambo as the locomotive on the daily mixed train from Ballinamore is serviced for the rest of its journey to Arigna. The locomotive is being replenished from a long pipe, the 5,000-gallon tank being located on the other side of the passing loop.**
Harry Luff / Online Transport Archive

Above: **With the GNR branch from Ballyhaise on the right, this picture taken at Belturbet on 27 April 1956 sees ex-Cork, Blackrock & Passage Railway 2-4-2T No 10L awaiting departure with the 4.00pm to Dromod. Following the closure of the CBPR in December 1932, the first locomotive to arrive on the C&L was No 13L in August 1934.**
J. Edgington

Below: **A detail side-on picture of Kerr-Stuart 2-6-0T No 4T at Dromod. Together with classmate No 3T, this locomotive was transferred from the Tralee & Dingle Railway during World War 2. Then, with the complete closure of the T&D in 1953, the remaining locomotives found their way to the C&L.** *Colour-Rail*

Above: **CDRJC 2-6-4T No 4** *Meenglas* **is captured between the platforms at Donegal Town station in May 1959. Following closure of the system in 1959** *Meenglas* **was purchased by the American Dr Cox in 1960 and after lying at Strabane for many years it had suffered heavily at the hands of vandals. Today it is present at the Foyle Valley Railway at Derry and may one day be returned to steam.**

Below: **Another picture of** *Meenglas* **taken earlier the same evening looking east from Donegal Town station. Behind the fine array of signals the Stranorlar line diverges to the left and the line to Ballyshannon to the right. Today the Heritage Centre of County Donegal Railway Restoration Ltd is located here, whose ambition is to operate some of the original locomotives and railcars.** *Derek Penney (both)*

Top: A general view at Stranorlar in May 1959 as *Meenglas* shunts wagons up to the goods store; the fine gantry signal and light can be clearly seen. A pile of sleepers on the left has been dumped in front of the carpenters' shops with the green door. Today, little in this picture has survived the intervening years with the exception of two faces of the station clock which have been preserved and mounted on a plinth in front of the church. *Derek Penney*

Above: An excellent view of the shed at Stranorlar taken on 8 May 1957. From left to right the three buildings with pitched roofs are the machine shop, railcar running shed and locomotive repair shop. *T. B. Owen*

Right: Railcar No 10 is seen in the platform at Stranorlar on 8 May 1957. Built by Walker Bros in 1932, it was the first articulated railcar to run in Ireland. Purchased by the CDRJC from the Clogher Valley Railway when it closed in 1941/2, it was given the number 10. Happily today it survives in the Ulster Folk & Transport Museum. *T. B. Owen*

Below: **Railcar No 20 is seen arriving at Strabane from Letterkenny in May 1959. The train has crossed the border bridge as it came in from Lifford in County Donegal into County Tyrone. Both railcars Nos 19 and 20 are on the Isle of Man Railway, although neither has run for a number of years.**

Bottom: **The signalbox at the north end of the GN platform can be seen on the right of this picture as 2-6-4T No 2 *Blanche* shunts stock at Strabane in May 1959. Diverging to the left is the former line to Derry, and the grey building above the wagons is the transhipment shed with facilities for wagons of both gauges in the sidings.** *Derek Penney (both)*

Above: **Another view of *Blanche* taken at Strabane in May 1959 with GNR Class S2 4-4-0 *Lugnaquilla* in the standard-gauge platform. The three Class S2 loconotives were delivered from Beyer Peacock in 1915, but were extensively rebuilt in 1938/9 and named after Irish mountains.** *Derek Penney*

Below: **Built for the Clogher Valley Railway as a steam locomotive with a vertical boiler, No 11 *Phœnix* was converted to a diesel tractor at the instruction of Henry Forbes, General Manager of the CDR, in 1932. The name *Phœnix* was given as acknowledgement of its return and again survives at Cultra.** *Harry Luff / Online Transport Archive*

Above: **A lengthy CDR goods train is preparing to leave Letterkenny hauled by an unidentified Class 5 locomotive on 12 September 1959. On the right railcar No 16 awaits its next turn of duty. The luggage rack on top of No 16 should be noted; these were generally only used for bicycles.**
J. Carter

Below: **A final picture on the CDR as Class 5 2-6-4T No 6 *Columbkille* is seen shunting at Letterkenny on 6 June 1957. Introduced in 1907, No 6 was originally No 18 *Killybegs* and became No 6 *Columbkille* in 1937. Despite being another victim of Dr Cox's scheme and languishing at Strabane, it finally joined *Meenglas* at the Foyle Valley Railway.**
T. B. Owen

Left: West Clare Railway's Walker Bo-Bo No F503 is depicted at Ennis in July 1957. Having 230bhp these locomotives were designated power class F midway between the 130hp Deutz 0-4-0s (G601-3) and the 420hp Maybach 0-6-0 shunters (E401-19). Weighing 23 tons, they were equipped with Gardner engines with mechanical transmission. *Colour-Rail*

Left: Originating on the Tralee & Dingle Railway this little four-wheeled inspection car lies derelict at Ennis in May 1959. It saw use on several of the GSR's narrow-gauge lines, being transported by broad-gauge wagon from one to another. This Ford-engined vehicle spent its last decade on the West Clare Railway. *Derek Penney*

Below: Four months after closure West Clare Railway's railcar No 3389 is depicted at Ennis in June 1961. Two years earlier this car had arrived back from Inchicore in pristine condition and was easily identified by the black roof on its cab which it had received on that visit. *J. Edgington*

35

Sligo, Leitrim & Northern Counties

Acquired from the GNR in 1938, the SL&NCR's second railbus No 2A and its trailer are seen on the turntable at Sligo on 8 May 1957. Having begun life as a GNR AEC road bus it was given a completely new body for use on rail and fitted with a new diesel engine, acquiring the luggage trailer from railcar 'A' when it was withdrawn in March 1939. Both remained in use until the SL&NCR closed. *T. B. Owen*

Connecting the port of Sligo on the Atlantic coast with Enniskillen, the county town of Fermanagh, this line's single track was devoid of any branch lines. Enniskillen was an important junction on the Great Northern Railway's system and provided an outlet for the SLNCR's traffic which mainly consisted of cattle reared in the west of Ireland. These were then taken onwards to east coast ports and shipped to destinations on the other side of the Irish Sea.

This line was remarkable in many ways and held the distinction of being the last standard gauge public railway in the British Isles to retain its independence. None of its locomotives carried numbers and were known by name only and latterly these were all of the 0-6-4T variety, all being built by the same manufacturer — Beyer, Peacock of Manchester.

At the outset the line was promoted by landowners and prominent residents at the Sligo end of the route, all anxious to access the benefits that rail transport would bring to the area. The line was built from the Enniskillen end and was opened in stages; the first to be completed was the 12½ miles from Enniskillen to Belcoo which opened to passengers in March 1879. The following year saw the opening of the next five miles to Glenfarne, and services over the next 7½ miles to Manorhamilton began on 1 December 1880. Services over the 16½-mile section to Collooney began on 1 September 1881, but the final section to Carrignagat Junction with the MGWR was delayed until November 1882 because of difficulties with the construction of the bridge over the Owenmore River.

The first locomotives delivered to the SLNCR were two Avonside-built 0-6-2Ts which arrived in 1877. In 1882 came the first in the line of 0-6-4Ts from Beyer, Peacock, these engines starting off life in lined olive green livery with polished domes and chimney caps. Later a plain black livery was adopted which was also applied to the brasswork, although the borders and lettering of the nameplates were picked out in red. For a short period in the early days of the black livery, the company initials SL&NCR, on the tanks of the 0-6-4T locomotives; the ampersand was omitted on *Sir Henry*.

Between 1877 and 1951 a total of 13 new locomotives were built for the line, 10 of these

coming from Beyer, Peacock, two from Avonside and one from Hudswell-Clarke. Seven second-hand locomotives were acquired between 1897 and 1941, two from contractors and five from the GNR (I). Total rolling stock was at a peak in 1913 when there were 19 carriages, 13 'other passenger vehicles' and 201 freight wagons. Locomotive and wagon repairs were undertaken in the company's workshops at Manorhamilton, although renewal of fireboxes was undertaken at Dundalk.

Like the GNR(I), the CDR, the L&LSR, and the DN&GR, partition of Ireland in 1921 adversely affected the operations of the railway. Like them also, the SL&NCR faced increasing competition from road transport, and in 1932 it tried out a GNR (I) railcar on its line. This encouraged the Sligo, Leitrim to order its first railbus, A, in 1934 from the GN. Delivered in 1935, it was followed over the next few years by others. The livery of the railcar and railbuses was two-tone green with white roofs. Below the waistline was regent green, with olive green above separated by one or two black lines. The company's full initials were applied at waist level in shaded leaf transfers. The letter identification was shown, again by means of transfers, below the driver's window on the front of the railbuses, and, on the railcar, on the panel separating the two windows on the power unit and passenger saloon ends.

The carriage livery was maroon, unlined, with the company's full initials (SL&NCR), running number (preceded by No.) and class indication applied in shaded leaf transfers. The livery of goods stock was the customary grey with the company initials (latterly abbreviated as 'SLNC') and running number applied in white paint; the number appeared on the ends of the vehicles in addition to the sides.

Since the countryside crossed by the line was poor and sparsely populated, and despite the one-time intermittent heavy cattle traffic, it was never prosperous. Despite subsidies from both Governments either side of the border, in its last days it was the closure of the GNR(I)'s line through Enniskillen that determined its own closure, this coming on 1 October 1957.

This picture, taken from the Enniskillen end of Dromahair station, depicts
0-6-4T *Lough Erne* awaiting departure with a train for Enniskillen on 7 May
1957. The tri-composite coach behind the locomotive had a 1st First-class
compartment with a sliding door down the middle, one half for smoking and the
other non-smoking. *T. B. Owen*

Top: **Railcar No 2A is featured again, this time at Belcoo & Blacklion as a Sligo–Enniskillen working. From 1922 onwards when Belcoo remained in County Fermanagh and the village of Blacklion in Cavan became part of the Irish Free State, this station served two communities in two different states.** *H. Luff / Online Transport Archive*

Above: **Another view on the turntable at Sligo, this time depicting railcar B on 7 May 1957. Carrying the SL&NCR's two-tone green livery, it was acquired from Walker Bros in Wigan in 1947. For its time it was modern, comfortable and attractive looking and was well liked by both staff and passengers.** *T. B. Owen*

Great Northern

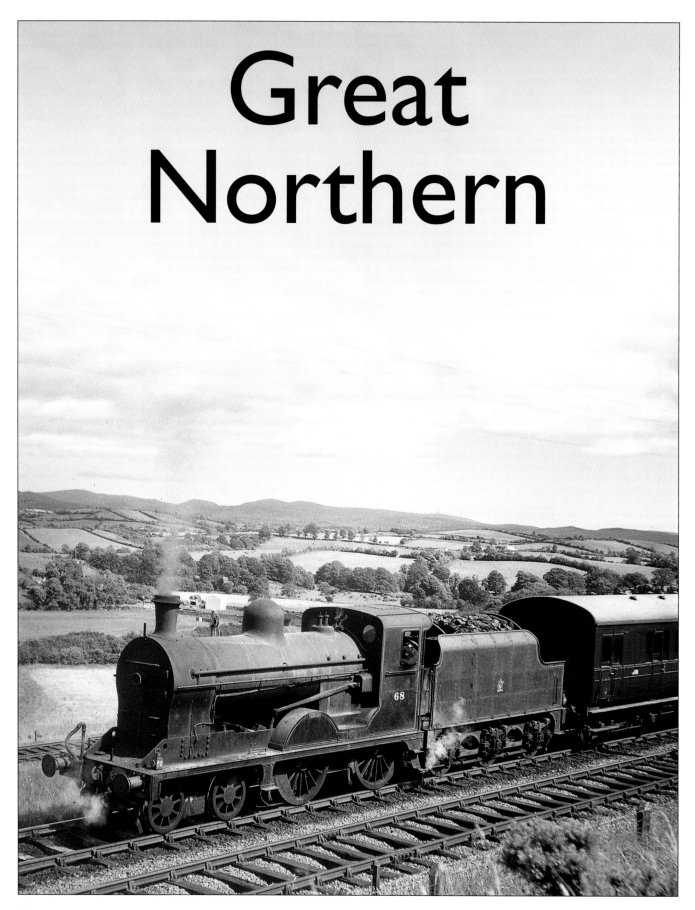

With the mountains of Mourne forming the backdrop this picture shows 'U' class 4-4-0 No 68 *Down* (ex-GNR No 205) standing on the up (to Dublin) line south of Goraghwood station with the stock of a Scarva 'Sham Fight' Demonstration special on Saturday 13 July 1963. *John Langford*

The Great Northern Railway (Ireland) was formed in 1876 by a merger of the Irish North Western Railway, Northern Railway of Ireland and the Ulster Railway, the latter being the GNR's oldest constituent, having opened between Belfast and Lisburn in 1839.

In its early years the GNR (I) had closely followed its English namesake with its locomotives wearing a pleasant green livery and its passenger coaches having a varnished teak finish. In later years the company adopted its famous pale blue livery for its passenger locomotives with the running gear and frames being picked out in scarlet.

In the early part of the 20th century an increase in traffic led the GNR (I) to consider the introduction of larger locomotives, the GSWR having already introduced locomotives with a 4-6-0 wheel arrangement for express passenger duties. Unfortunately the lifting shop in Dundalk Works was too short to build a 4-6-0 so the company had to continue the construction of 4-4-0 locomotives even for its heaviest and fastest passenger trains. This led to the order of the very powerful and modern Class V three-cylinder compounds built by Beyer, Peacock in 1932 which have been compared to the Southern Railway (of England) Class V 4-4-0s built in 1930.

The border created at partition of Ireland in 1921 crossed all three of the GNR(I)'s main lines and a number of its secondary routes. This caused the imposition of frontier controls and some disruption to services, trains from Belfast to Dublin having to stop at both Dundalk and Goraghwood. This situation was not eased until 1947 when Customs and immigration facilities were introduced at both Belfast Great Victoria Street and Dublin Amiens Street stations.

With both an increase in competition from road transport and the change in economic patterns caused by the partition of Ireland, the prosperity of the GNR(I)'s activities was reduced. In response to this, the company made improvements with the introduction of modern diesel multiple-units and a non-stop service between Belfast and Dublin in 1948. By the 1950s the GNR(I) had ceased to be profitable and was jointly nationalised by the Governments of the Republic of Ireland and Northern Ireland. The

two Governments ran the railway jointly under a Great Northern Railway Board until May 1958 when the Northern Ireland Government expressed its desire to close many lines, this leading to the GNR Board being dissolved and its assets divided between the two states. The control of all lines in Northern Ireland was transferred to the Ulster Transport Authority and all those in the Republic of Ireland to Córas Iompair Éireann.

In an attempt to be fair all classes of locomotives and rolling stock were divided equally between the new operators, but with most of the GNR(I) locomotives being built in small numbers, this division left both railways with maintenance problems.

Following this division the Northern Ireland Government rapidly closed all GNR(I) lines in Northern Ireland with the exception of the Belfast–Dundalk and the Portadown–Londonderry main lines in addition to the Newry–Warrenpoint and Lisburn–Antrim branches, the latter becoming freight only from 1960. By 1965 the Portadown–Derry and the Newry–Warrenpoint lines were closed to all traffic. The Republic of Ireland government briefly tried to continue services on lines closed at the border but this proved impractical and the Republic had to follow suit and close most secondary lines south of the border. The Hill of Howth Tramway in the northern suburbs of Dublin was also acquired by the CIE in 1958 but closed down in June 1959.

Today four GNR(I) steam locomotives survive in preservation. With its headquarters at Whitehead the Railway Preservation Society of Ireland owns three 4-4-0s, one each of Classes S, Q and V, which are periodically operated on excursion trains and enthusiasts' railtours on Northern Ireland Railways and Iarnrod Éireann (the successor to the CIE). A 2-4-2T locomotive is preserved at the Ulster Folk and Transport Museum at Cultra. Some of the GNR(I)'s passenger stock has also been preserved, the 1938-built dining car No 88 being part of the RPSI's 'Heritage Set'. Also operating in this set is 1954-built brake coach No 9 which currently carries the number 1949.

Top: A view outside Belfast Great Victoria Street station taken on 31 August 1964 as UTA 2-6-4T No 53 departs with a train for Dublin. Having four platforms under the cover of its overall train shed roof, the station had an additional short platform on its south side, known as the 'Motor platform.

Above: Also seen at Great Victoria Street station on 31 August 1964, careworn 'S' class 4-4-0 No 170 *Errigal* is captured on station pilot duties. Considered by some as the most beautifully proportioned and elegant 4-4-0s ever to grace an Irish railway, they were superb performers and were named after Irish mountains. *Alan Jarvis (both)*

Above: UTA 'Vs' class 4-4-0 No 58 *Lagan* (GN No 208) is seen at Belfast Adelaide shed in May 1959. The division of the GNR in 1958 meant that Nos 206/7/9 were allocated to the CIE and Nos 208/10 to the UTA.

Below: Another locomotive portrait at Adelaide in May 1959, this time showing UTA 'U' class 4-4-0 No 64 (GNR No 196) *Lough Gill* with its former GN letters on the tender having been removed.
Derek Penney (both)

Top: **UTA Class UG 0-6-0 No 47 is depicted against the coaling stage at Adelaide in May 1959. The first five of this class built at Dundalk in 1937 were the last new locomotives to be constructed there. Light and powerful. they were equally suited to both passenger and goods duties.** *Derek Penney*

Above: **UTA Class Vs 4-4-0 No 207** *Boyne* **is seen at Adelaide on 17 May 1964 before working an excursion train to Drogheda. In the foreground are the timbers used in conjunction with the open-air wheel drop. This allowed wheels to be dropped for attention to the bearings.** *M. Collins*

Top: Ex-NCC 2-6-0 No 97 *Earl of Ulster* is depicted passing Adelaide with a Dublin express in May 1958. Together with Nos 91/4/5/9 and 104, No 97 had been transferred to Belfast Adelaide shed to work on GNR territory, from Belfast to Dundalk and to Derry via Omagh principally on freight. Being the last member of the class to visit the shops, No 97 survived until withdrawal in December 1965. *Derek Penney*

Above: A general view of Adelaide shed taken on 1 September 1964. Situated on the down side of the main line, the shed at Adelaide was connected to Great Victoria Street station by the 1½-mile-long 'third road'. Under permissive block working light engines and goods trains could be operated in either direction. The nine parallel roads could accommodate 55 locomotives, but in January 1950 its allocation was 72. *Alan Jarvis*

Top: Repainted in UTA lined black livery and renumbered, 'U' class 4-4-0 No 67 (GNR No 202) *Louth* is seen at Lambeg station with the 8.0am Portadown-Belfast on 19 May 1964. The first five members of this class were built in 1915 and were un-named, then 33 years later in 1948 another five were constructed.

Above: Built in July 1958, former GNR three-car DMU No 131 draws to a halt at Lambeg station on 19 May 1964 as the 8.28am Belfast–Lisburn; a number of passengers including several school children are waiting to board. *Derrick Codling (both)*

Right: **A former GNR four-car DMU forms the 8.30am Portadown–Belfast service at Lambeg on 19 May 1964. The 'V'-shaped stripes painted on the fronts of railcars closely followed BR experiments to make them more conspicuous to track workmen, these being introduced on both former NCC and GN lines in September 1960.**
Derrick Codling

Above: **UTA 'U' class 4-4-0 No 67** *Louth* **is depicted again as it approaches Lambeg with an evening commuter train from Belfast on 18 May 1964. The five 1915-built members of this class were given names of loughs between 1949 and 1953. It could be remarked that the formation down the Lagan Valley towards Lisburn was wider than normal, which was due to the fact that the original Ulster Railway was built to a gauge of 6ft 2in.** *M. Collins*

Right: **A final view of Lambeg station taken on 19 May 1964 as UTA two-car DMU No 7 arrives as the 9.50am Belfast–Lisburn. This AEC-built unit was constructed in August 1951 and was last used in service on 15 July 1966. It met its end at Belfast York Road when it was burned on 18 November 1969.** *Derrick Codling*

Top: **UTA Class Vs 4-4-0 No 207** *Boyne* **runs round its train at Lisburn on 31 August 1964. One of a handful of locomotives kept in reserve for the summer of 1965, No 207 worked a railtour on 11 September, after which it was put into store and in due course cut up at Adelaide.** *Alan Jarvis*

Above: **Built for the GNR (I) in 1947 by Beyer, Peacock of Manchester, Class UG 0-6-0 No 49 is depicted on shed at Portadown on 19 May 1964. With slight modifications this was perpetuating a GN mixed-traffic design of 1937.** *Derrick Codling*

Top: **Situated between the lines to Dublin and Clones, the roundhouse at Portadown is pictured here on 23 August 1963. It was one of two roundhouses on the GN, the other being at Clones, both being constructed from reinforced concrete. After Portadown shed closed in 1965 its eventual demolition was carried out by the Army using explosives.** *Neville Fields*

Above: **Former 'GN' class 4-4-0 No 172, now UTA No 60** *Slieve Donard* **heads a southbound departure from Portadown across the River Bann bridge on 31 August 1964. The station shown here was the third to be built at Portadown and was opened in July 1863. A new station called Craigavon West replacing the one seen here was opened in October 1970, but the name was soon changed to 'Portadown'.** *Alan Jarvis*

Above: **A somewhat work-stained GN 'S' class 4-4-0 No 174** *Carrantuohill* **approaches Dungannon with a Londonderry–Belfast train on 1 September 1964. The five 'S' class locomotives delivered by Beyer, Peacock in 1913 were the top main-line passenger locomotives before the advent of the Compounds which were introduced in 1932.** *Alan Jarvis*

Below: **GNR 'JT' class 2-4-2T No 91 is seen on 4 June 1957 as it leaves Belturbet for Ballyhaise. Six of this class were built at Dundalk between 1895 and 1902 and were an early form of motive power for branch line and local trains. Today, sister locomotive No 93 survives in the museum at Cultra.** *T. B. Owen*

Left: Spending much of its life working on the Irish North, Railcar No C1 is depicted on shed at Enniskillen on 7 May 1957. Like the CDR railcars the driving compartment containing the engine was articulated from the passenger saloon. Built at Dundalk in 1934, this vehicle remained in traffic until September 1961. *T. B. Owen*

Left: 1950s-built AEC railcars Nos 616/7 sandwich their centre trailer in this picture taken at Enniskillen in August 1956. AEC had been building railcars for the Great Western Railway in England before the war and had developed a control system enabling two power cars to be driven by one driver. Years ahead of their time, the GNR foresaw the day when all passenger services would be operated by this type of unit. *Colour-Rail*

Below: GNR 'U' class 4-4-0 No 199 *Lough Derg* waits for departure from Enniskillen with a train for Clones on 7 May 1957. This and classmate No 197 *Lough Neagh* were the first two locomotives of the five constructed in 1915 to receive names between 1949 and 1953. *T. B. Owen*

Above: '**Dick**' is being manoeuvred into position for a departure from Fintona Junction for Fintona on 8 May 1957. In January 1953 the 'engine' got out of control and the tram was damaged. So great was the local agitation the tram was repaired and the town of Fintona turned out to give it a great welcome on its return in May 1953.

Below: When the Londonderry & Enniskillen Railway was extended from Fintona to Enniskillen in 1854 Fintona was left at the end of a ½-mile branch. Since then the passenger traffic was always worked by a horse tram, the normal goods train serving Fintona each day. Now preserved in the museum at Cultra, the tram was estimated to have travelled 125,000 miles on the branch. *T. B. Owen (both)*

Above: **One of five 'SGs' built by Beyer, Peacock in 1913, GN 0-6-0 No 175 is seen with a freight at Londonderry on 6 June 1957. A second batch of 10 'SG2s' was built between 1915 and 1925.** *T. B. Owen*

Below: **UTA 'S2' class 4-4-0 No 63 *Slievenamon* is seen on shed at Derry on 24 August 1963. The closure of the Derry Road in February 1965 leaves a huge gap in the railway map of Ireland.** *Neville Fields*

Top: **GN 'U' class 4-4-0 No 205** *Down* **awaits departure from Clones with the 'Bundoran Express' in August 1956. Running daily in summer between Dublin and Bundoran, this train crossed the border several times, a third of its journey being in Northern Ireland. With no scheduled stops in the North, no Customs examinations were necessary.**
Colour-Rail

Above: **No 205** *Down* **is depicted again as UTA No 68, this time on 13 July 1963 at Poyntzpass where it is at the head of the 1.30pm Portadown–Warrenpoint. This was a booked train, not a special, and was a connection at Portadown with the 12.30pm Belfast–Dublin.**
John Langford

54

Above: Photographed from the top of the quarry at Goraghwood, GN Class SG3 0-6-0 No 36 (GN No 49) awaits departure with a lengthy freight in May 1963. With the break-up of the GNR in 1958 eight of this class went to the UTA and seven to CIE. Shopped at York Road instead of Dundalk, they appeared lined out in red and straw. *Colour-Rail*

Below: UTA 2-6-4T No 53 awaits Customs clearance at Goraghwood with a Dublin train on 2 September 1964. Most trains stopped here for Customs clearance excepting the 'Enterprise' where examinations took place at either terminus, allowing non-stop runs between Belfast and Dublin. *Alan Jarvis*

Top: **With the station's polychromatic brickwork and yellow and black signs this picture presents a classic GN scene at Warrenpoint on 19 May 1964 as UTA Class SG2 0-6-0 No 40 (GN No 18) waits for departure with the empty coaching stock of the 3.50pm from Newry.** *Derrick Codling*

Above: **Another picture at Warrenpoint: this time UTA 4-4-0 (GNR No 201) No 66 *Meath* reverses into the platform on 31 August 1964. As a seaside town Warrenpoint attracted a good number of day trippers, trains often being strengthened to cope with additional passengers who wanted to take the sea air.** *Alan Jarvis*

Top: UTA Class Vs 4-4-0 No 207 *Boyne* passes the signal cabin at Mount Pleasant on the climb to Adavoyle with a Dublin–Belfast train in August 1964. Most of the 8½-mile climb to a gap in the hills on the border is at nearly 1 in 100. *Colour-Rail*

Above: This classic portrait of GNR Class V Compound 4-4-0 No 85 *Merlin* was taken outside Dundalk shed in May 1959. When built in 1932, it was one of five locomotives constructed to the first new Compound design in the British Isles for some 30 years. *Derek Penney*

Below: Taken from the down platform at Drogheda, looking south towards the trailing junction with the Navan & Oldcastle branch, this picture shows 'A' class diesel No A41 in green livery at work on station pilot duties on 12 August 1963. *John Langford*

Bottom: Seen at Dublin Amiens Street shed in June 1961 is the GSR's second attempt at a general-duties 0-6-0, the superheated Class 710 (J15b) No 719. Built in 1929 as an addition to the '101' class, it did not compare favourably with the older design. *Derek Penney*

Above: **The last survivor of five members of Class I3, 0-6-2T No 673 is depicted outside Dublin Amiens Street shed in June 1961. Built as Class 670 by the GSR in 1933/4, they represented a final attempt by the GSR to introduce a tank locomotive specifically for the Dublin–Bray– Greystones commuter services.** *T. B. Owen*

Below: **Green-liveried Co-Co 'A' class diesel No A46 is captured in this scene outside Dublin Amiens Street shed in June 1959. Introduced by the CIE in 1955, these locomotives were powered by a two-stroke type that Crossley Bros had been manufacturing for many years. With a maximum power of 1,200hp the unit was an eight-cylinder 'V' formation.** *Colour-Rail*

Above: GNR 'Q' class 4-4-0 No 132 is portrayed outside Dublin Amiens Street shed in June 1961. Whilst earlier GNR 4-4-0s were ideally suited for working on secondary routes, something more powerful for the main lines was required. Clifford's solution was the 13 'Q' class locomotives built between 1899 and 1904. *Derek Penney*

Below: An earlier picture taken at Amiens Street shed in May 1959 depicts the now preserved sister 'Q' class locomotive No 131 on the turntable. These bigger and more powerful types were considered the equal of any similar machines in use on the other side of the Irish Sea at that time. *Colour-Rail*

Above: **Hill of Howth tram No 4 is seen outside the depot on 15 March 1959. This 5¼-mile line between Sutton and Howth was opened by the GN in 1901 and climbed to a height of 407ft before descending back to sea level, long sections of the line being at a gradient of 1 in 20. Eight of the passenger cars carried the GN blue livery, the other two being in teak.** *John Langford*

Below: **Teak-liveried car No 9 is depicted inside the shed at Sutton on 5 May 1957. Closing on 31 May 1959, the service was replaced by CIE buses. Of the 10 cars in operation four are preserved, two in Ireland, one at the National Tramway Museum at Crich and another in California.** *T. B. Owen*

Midland Great Western

Top: **On the last day of operation on the Kilfree Junction–Ballaghaderreen branch, 2 February 1963, MGWR 0-6-0 No 574 approaches Island Road with one of the final workings.** *R. Hobbs*

Above: **CIE Class B diesel No B158 is captured by Athlone West Junction cabin in 1961. The MGWR main line crossed the Shannon at Athlone by a bridge 542ft long with opening centre span.** *J. Edgington*

With 538 route miles the Midland Great Western Railway was third in size among the railways of Ireland. It was not far behind the GNR(I) with 617 miles but both fell far short of the Great Southern & Western Railway with its 1,150 miles.

The MGWR system extended across the Midlands with its main line running from Dublin to Galway, a distance of 126½ miles. To the south of this main line there were only three short branches, to Edenderry, Clara and Loughrea, but to the north there were the long branches to Sligo and Westport which were secondary main lines. As well as these, further branches and extensions completed the system.

The first section of the MGWR to be opened was that from Dublin to Enfield on 28 June 1847. By 2 October 1848 the line had been completed as far as Mullingar. The final 76 miles from Mullingar to Galway were opened on 1 August 1851, the principal engineering work on this section being the bridge over the Shannon at Athlone, wich was 542ft long with an opening centre span.

The headquarters, works and largest locomotive depot were at Broadstone in Dublin. Dublin was a city of fine station buildings and Broadstone was one of them, its architect being John Skipton Mulvany who also designed Athlone, Galway and other smaller stations on the main line. Behind the station building was the train shed with just two platforms and four sidings between them.

The works and locomotive depot functioned from the start and grew over the years. The first locomotives were built when Martin Atock became Locomotive Superintendent in 1872, and by the time the last one had been completed in 1927 some 126 had been constructed there. Until 1905 the MGWR painted its locomotives in a bright green colour, after which there was an experimental but short-lived dark blue livery used on some of them. With this livery not wearing well the company reverted to green until taken over by the GSR which introduced its dull grey livery, followed by the un-lined black of CIE. Passenger coaches were finished in varnish or brown paint until the advent of the blue livery. As with the locomotives this was so short-lived that very few

vehicles were painted this colour. The company then reverted to brown, though after 1910 lining out was seldom applied. In 1918 a very dark crimson was used, this lasting until GSR days and beyond, as it was very similar to the GSR's own livery.

Following the amalgamation of 1925 the GSR had no long-term future for Broadstone, having stations at Amiens Street and Westland Row which could handle all the traffic and were more convenient for the city.

With the routes of the MGWR concentrated in the flat lands of central Ireland which offered none of the challenges faced by the GSWR there was no incentive to construct larger locomotives. With a degree of standardisation the company's needs were achieved by the construction of 14 basic classes. The use of modern engineering practices resulted in a higher proportion of locomotives being superheated than in any other Irish company. Had it not been for the amalgamation the decision to acquire 12 Woolwich Moguls would have given the company a class of the most modern machines then available. At the time of the amalgamation the MGWR had 139 locomotives, these being renumbered 530 to 668 by the GSR they were re-designated under the new classification system. At the formation of the CIE in 1945 all but 20 were still running; no further renumbering took place.

Today the diesel reigns supreme and all the MGWR branch lines except that to Ballina have been closed. However, much of the system remains to be seen — the Dublin–Galway main line, though currently out of use between Mullingar and Athlone, as Galway and Mayo trains use the former GSWR route to Athlone, the Mullingar–Sligo line and the Mayo line from Athlone to Westport, a total of over 300 miles. So the Midland Line, as it is often called, is still very much extant.

Unfortunately no MGWR locomotives have survived into preservation. However, several examples of its standard six-wheeled carriages still exist. One lies derelict at the Station House Hotel in Clifden, another three are on the Downpatrick & County Down Railway, whilst another which is owned by the RPSI is undergoing refurbishment for public use on the Downpatrick line.

Top: **Class K1a 'Woolwich' 2-6-0 Mogul No 396 receives attention at Broadstone in May 1950. The 12 kits purchased by the MGWR were assembled at the Broadstone Works (locomotives Nos 372-83); the 15 GSR sets of parts forming only 14 locomotives were assembled at Inchicore (locomotives Nos 384-98 — No 392 was blank).**

Bottom: **Another picture taken at Broadstone, this time showing former DSER 2-6-0 No 462 in August 1955. One of two members of the class, sister locomotive No 461 being preserved by the RPSI, they were the only DSER locomotives to carry superheaters throughout their existence. No 462 is seen here fitted with ash chutes to the smokebox.**
Colour-Rail (both)

Above: **GNR 'Q' class 4-4-0 No 132 is seen here with an IRRS railtour at Kingscourt on 3 June 1961. At Kingscourt this line was just half a mile into Co Cavan and was known as the 'Meath Road'. On the left of the picture are wagons containing gypsum which was mined locally.**
Ray Reed

Below: **Also on the line to Kingscourt we see another railtour, this time hauled by GN Class UG 0-6-0 No 49, captured at Nobber on 14 May 1966. This locomotive was built in 1947 by Beyer, Peacock of Manchester to a GN design of 1937 with slight modifications, having 5ft 1in driving wheels and a tractive effort of 21,600lb.** *J. Edgington*

Top: **Also on railtour duty former GSWR 'J15' 0-6-0 No 184 is seen at Enfield on 9 June 1961. Together with former DSER 2-6-0 No 461, No 184 is on permanent loan to the Railway Preservation Society of Ireland under an agreement made with Córas Iompair Éireann in 1977.** *T. B. Owen*

Above: **The IRRS organised two 'outings' to Kingscourt, on Saturdays 3 and 10 July 1965, using railcar No 2509 which CIE had purchased from the liquidators of the SLNCR, on which it was railcar B. Here it is seen on the 'Meath Road' at Wilkinstown on 10 July 1965. It now awaits restoration at Downpatrick.** *John Langford*

Above: **A delightful late evening study of former MGWR Class D6 4-4-0 No 541 at Athlone in June 1957. In 1938 this locomotive was identified to be carrying a boiler from a Class F 0-6-0 by virtue of it still being equipped with connections for the ex-MGWR track-laying machine.** *Colour-Rail*

Below: **Former MGWR Class J18 0-6-0 No 592 shunts a Post Office Sorting Van at Mullingar on 6 May 1957. The latter was one of four similar vehicles built to the design of Mr Atock in 1888 and ran as GSR No 3M.** *T. B. Owen*

Below: **A panoramic view looking east at Attymon Junction taken in June 1962. The station house can be seen in this picture sited at right angles between main line and branch platforms. It is a single-storey brick-built structure with waiting room, booking office, parcels office and ladies' room. For the stationmaster were three bedrooms, sitting room, kitchen, outside toilet and fuel store.** *Roy Hobbs*

Bottom: **Former MGWR Class J19 0-6-0 No 610 is seen at Attymon Junction on 7 June 1961 having arrived from Loughrea. It will return as the 12.05pm mixed train to Loughrea. Until well into the 1960s the original MGWR vitrolite sign stating 'Change here for Dunsandle and Loughrea' still survived on the main-line platform.** *Neville Simms*

Above: On remote Irish branch lines in the 1960s it was not unusual to be 'invited up'. Here, taken from the cab of Deutz 4-wheeled diesel No G613 on 31 August 1965, the 10.50am from Loughrea to Attymon Junction, approaches one of the several manned crossings on the line. The Permanent Way Inspector was driving the locomotive at this stage.

Below: The only passenger trains to be regularly hauled by Deutz four-wheeled diesels were on the Loughrea branch in Co Galway. No G613 is seen at the terminus at Loughrea on 31 August 1965. Loughrea was an important cattle and sheep centre; animals sold at the great fairs held in the town often left by rail. *John Langford (both)*

Top: The branch from Attymon Junction to Loughrea and the Ballinrobe–Claremorris line were both Baronial Lines built by the MGWR. Here CIE Class J18 0-6-0 No 590 heads out of Ballinrobe for Claremorris on 5 June 1957.

Above: Another view of No 590 on the same day as it stands in the platform at Ballinrobe. The branch was closed to all traffic from 1 January 1960, the service of two trains per day being replaced by diversion of the Westport–Longford bus to call at Ballinrobe in each direction. *T. B. Owen (both)*

Top: **CIE Metrovick Class A Co-Co diesel No A14 is seen on the turntable at Galway on 31 August 1965. These locomotives did not normally require turning but in this case the driver's cab heating was only working at one end! Beyond the locomotive two vintage items of departmental stock stand on the remnant of the long branch to Clifden, closed in 1935.** *John Langford*

Above: **Former MGWR Class J19 0-6-0 No 610 is seen as it awaits departure from Edmondstown on the Kilfree Junction–Ballaghaderreen branch in October 1962. If some 1850s schemes had come to fruition Ballaghaderreen would have been on a through line, but was eventually connected to the Sligo line at Kilfree Junction.** *Roy Hobbs*

Right: Class G2 2-4-0 No 655 is seen at Ballaghaderreen in May 1957 as rebuilt with round-topped superheated boiler and modern cab. Considered by many to be the best of all MGWR designs, by the 1960s they were among the last 2-4-0s at work anywhere in the world. *Colour-Rail*

Above: A general view at Ballaghaderreen looking towards Kilfree Junction on 4 February 1963 as MGWR Class J18 No 574 has arrived with a train from Kilfree Junction. This was the last day of services on the branch, the lifting of the track being carried out very shortly after closure by a private contractor who removed rails and sleepers at the Ballaghaderreen end using road vehicles. *R. Hobbs*

Left: Class G2 2-4-0 No 655 is seen passing the goods shed at Ballaghaderreen on 8 June 1961 before turning and taking the 11.50am back to Kilfree Junction. This class were Atock's standard passenger locomotives built at Broadstone from 1893-8; a larger-wheeled version for Limited Mail trains dated from 1889 but at this time they were long since scrapped. *Derek Penney*

Above: CIE Class B diesel No B132 has come to the rescue of the IRRS/ SLS/RCTS railtour, having replaced failed CIE Class J19 0-6-0 No 603 at Sligo, and is seen here at Kilfree Junction on 8 June 1961. No 603 had suffered a cracked cylinder cover, whilst No B132 had been shunting on Sligo Quay. *Derek Penney*

Below: CIE Class C diesel No C209 has arrived at Foxford with a train from Ballina to Manulla Junction on 5 June 1957. Always an important branch, the 20-mile Ballina line was opened to Foxford in 1870 and extended to Ballina in 1873. The extension to Killala was opened in 1893 and was the first of these lines to close in 1931. *T. B. Owen*

Great Southern & Western

A quintessentially Irish railway picture taken on the former GSWR line between Mallow and Waterford. With a backdrop of the Knockmealdown Mountains CIE Class J15 0-6-0 No 109 heads a sugar beet working between Cappoquin and Cappagh in October 1962. *Roy Hobbs*

One of the main railway operations in Ireland, the Great Southern & Western Railway was the largest of Ireland's 'Big Four' railway operators having bought up smaller concerns and expanded its route mileage for much of its existence.

GSWR headquarters was Dublin Kingsbridge (now Heuston) and the heart of operations was the Cork main line, a route still important today. The company also worked the main routes to Kilkenny, Waterford, Limerick and Tralee, as well as the long cross-country line from/to Mallow via Waterford. In the west the GSWR and MGWR territory became more or less self-contained, though there was early conflict north of Limerick.

The GSWR's purchase of the Waterford, Limerick & Western Railway in 1901 brought the cross-country route from Waterford to Collooney via Limerick, Athenry and Claremorris as well as the North Kerry line under its umbrella. The WLWR, recently named the Western Rail Corridor, ran right through MGWR territory, but it did however complement the radial MGWR lines from Dublin, allowing for traffic from Limerick to Galway and from Galway to Sligo, and connected intermediate destinations in the west of Ireland.

In 1925 the GSWR together with all the other railways operating wholly within the Irish Free State was amalgamated to form the Great Southern Railways, cross-border railways being excluded. Further amalgamation took place in 1945 with the Grand Canal Co and the Dublin United Tramway Co to form Córas Iompair Éireann, the Irish State Transport Co which was later nationalised in 1950. CIE remained in operation until 1987 when it was broken up into separate road and rail interests, and from then until today the railways are operated by Irish Rail (Iarnrod Éireann).

As with other railways in Ireland, in its early days the GSWR purchased its locomotives from private suppliers until its own works at Inchicore became operational in 1852, when it was able to supply most of the company's needs. Apart from some 0-6-0s

acquired from the WL&WR all freight requirements were covered by the ubiquitous Class 101 until the 1900s when some larger designs were introduced. The company made extensive use of 4-4-0s for main line and secondary passenger services, a wheel arrangement introduced to Ireland by McDonnell in 1877 as an advance on the existing 2-4-0s. The relatively long distances covered by many of the GSWR secondary services and the poor water quality at many stations precluded the use of tank locomotives. When they were used for branch or secondary passenger services they were mainly of the 2-4-2T, 4-4-2T and 0-4-4T wheel arrangements, some of these types enjoying relatively long lives. In the late 19th century, the GSWR livery for locomotives was quite exotic, some being painted in olive green with lining in red/yellow/red. The Coey years saw the livery changed to overall black lined out with white and red, this continuing until World War 1.

Standard livery for passenger stock was a dark shade of purple lake with lines of yellow and vermilion, lettering being gold with red shading. In the early 1900s some coaches had upper cream panels. The crest, incorporating the arms of Dublin, Cork, Kilkenny and Limerick, appeared on the side of all coaching stock.

At the formation of the GSR, the largest constituent locomotive fleet was that from the GSWR and no renumbering of locomotives took place. The GSR also operated a fleet of departmental service locomotives, some of which were switched back and forth between departmental and service stock as required. In 1925 one source stated that there were 12 locomotives listed in this category — six 0-6-0s, one 0-6-4T, one 0-6-0T, one 0-4-4T and three 0-4-2Ts.

Of the former independent rail operators in Ireland's railway history the GSWR is perhaps the best remembered, the routes which remain being some of the most heavily used in Ireland, connecting Dublin to Limerick, Cork and Waterford, the coats of arms of these cities decorating the façade of Heuston station to this day.

Left: Rebuilt Class B2a 4-6-0 No 406 is portrayed at Inchicore in August 1955. In 1930 No 406 together with No 401 were rebuilt with two cylinders. In both cases Beardmore-Caprotti valve gear was adopted giving infinitely variable cut-off. The benefits gained from this rebuild were reflected in the mileages achieved by No 406. Over the years from 1921-30 it ran a mere 60,318 miles in its four-cylinder condition but in the following 10 years it achieved a substantial 334,257 miles. *Colour-Rail*

Left: Another view taken at Inchicore depicts Class F6 2-4-2T No 42 on 3 June 1961. The last member of the class surviving in use at that time, No 42 was one of three locomotives built between 1892 and 1894 for service on the Kerry branch lines. *T. B. Owen*

Below: A general view of North Wall depot in Dublin recorded in June 1962. Established by the LNWR in the 1870s, North Wall once had a passenger service, although this was withdrawn as early as 1922. Upgraded with new cranes in 1970 and 1994, it was the withdrawal of container traffic that resulted in its closure in 2005. Adjacent to the LNWR yard was the MGWR goods yard which was also used for loading containers but by forklift, this too closing in 2005, the new Docklands station now standing on part of the site. *Roy Hobbs*

Above: Reputedly assembled mainly out of spare parts and employed as Inchicore Works shunter, Class L2 *Sambo* is seen on 3 June 1961. Its short wheelbase allowed it to operate over sharp curves around the works. *T. B. Owen*

Below: Built by CIE at Inchicore Works in 1957, the 14 Class E diesels were fitted with Maybach engines and transmissions. Used for shunting and transfer duties, No E402 is seen at Inchicore on 9 June 1961. *Neville Simms*

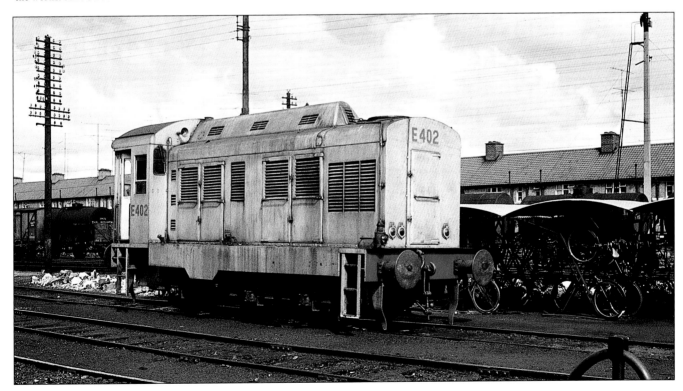

Above: **This picture shows former GSR Class D4 4-4-0 No 346 at Dublin Kingsbridge in 1957. In 1946 No 346 had been sent on loan to the GNR to work the 'Bundoran Express' between Dublin and Dundalk to assess the design of the planned Class Vs three-cylinder 4-4-0s which were to be introduced the following year.**

Below: **Immaculately clean ex-GSWR Class D2 4-4-0 No 329 is seen at Inchicore in April 1957. In 1928 No 329 is reputed to have worked a five- bogie special from Limerick Junction to Kingsbridge, covering the 107 miles in 104 minutes just using the contents of a 3,345-gallon tender.**
Colour-Rail (both)

Left: End of the line at Mountmellick — though the Waterford & Central Ireland Railway had once sought to reach north to Mullingar. In very worn original silver livery Class A diesel No A28 runs round an empty sugar beet special from the Thurles Sugar Factory on 18 December 1959. The Beet Campaign, operating each year from October to January, brought life to several branch lines otherwise dormant for most of the year. *John Langford*

Left: With the headboard removed CIE Class J15 0-6-0 No 125 is seen with the IRRS/SLS/RCTS railtour at Ballybrophy on 6 June 1961. The 119 members of the 'J15' class were built between 1866 and 1903, 20 locomotives being supplied by outside contractors (Beyer, Peacock 12, Sharp-Stewart 8). Two members of the class are now preserved, Nos 184 and 186. While No 184 is saturated and in virtually original condition, No 186 is superheated. *Derek Penney*

Below: Green-liveried CIE railcar set No 2602 prepares to leave Limerick station in March 1961. *Colour-Rail*

Top: **A view taken inside the erecting shop at Limerick Works on 7 June 1961. Situated in the triangle at Limerick, the works had been the headquarters of the Waterford, Limerick & Western Railway. In its day it was managed by some well known engineers including Martin Atock and John Robinson.** *T. B. Owen*

Above: **Despite extensive dieselisation of most regular passenger and goods trains by 1959, some steam could still be found on branch-line workings and shunting, including this ancient Class J15 0-6-0 No 134 shunting at Waterford West on 17 December 1959.** *John Langford*

Right: **Former DESR Class K2 2-6-0 No 461 reverses into the west end of Waterford station onto the stock of the IRRS/SLS/RCTS railtour on 6 June 1961. The girders that can be seen behind the overbridge support the Waterford signal cabin.** *Derek Penney*

Above: **CIE Class J15 0-6-0 No 116 works a local train from Rosslare Harbour to Wexford North in September 1958. The train has left Wexford South station and will come onto the quayside section.**

Right: **Work-stained CIE Class A diesel No A54 passes Wexford South signal cabin with a Wexford North–Rosslare Harbour train, also in September 1958. The Class A diesels were ordered from Metropolitan-Vickers as part of a contract worth £4,750,000 for the supply of 94 diesel-electric locomotives to CIE. The first of this class to be delivered arrived in the summer of 1955 and was initially diagrammed to work between Dublin and Cork.** *D. Cross (both)*

81

Above: **CIE Class J9 0-6-0 No 351 is seen running tender-first on Wexford Quay in September 1959. No 351 was constructed in 1903 and survived until 1963. Sister locomotive No 353 was withdrawn in 1930 as a result of damage sustained in a collision at Monasterevan.** *D. Cross*

Below: **Former DSER Class K2 2-6-0 No 461 is seen again with the IRRS/SLS/RCTS tour on 6 June 1961 at Fermoy, between Dungarvan and Mallow. All train services over the 73½-mile Waterford–Mallow line were withdrawn on 25 March 1967.** *Derek Penney*

Above: **Recently re-painted in CIE green livery, Class A diesel No A19 was photographed at Mallow on 4 June 1961. The dieselisation of the CIE system had been achieved gradually since 1952 when the first of the familiar AEC railcar sets was delivered.** *R. Reed*

Below: **Silver-liveried CIE Class G 4-wheeled diesel No G601 is seen at Banteer with a Newmarket goods working in May 1958. Except for a monthly livestock train this branch had been nominally closed between January 1947 and 1956, when it was reopened to goods traffic.** *J. Edgington*

Right: **Seen at Tralee on 5 June 1961 CIE Class J26 0-6-0T No 560 is waiting to take two of the five coaches from the IRRS/SLS/RCTS tour along the north of Tralee Bay to Fenit. One of Martin Atock's small tank engines built for working short branch lines, No 560 was built for the MGWR by Kitson in 1894. The cab and footsteps were altered in 1932 for use on the Waterford & Tramore section, and with its dieselisation No 560 was sent to Tralee for working Fenit Pier.** *Derek Penney*

Above: **On Sunday 29 August 1965 happy day trippers spread out over the grass-grown platform at Fenit (closed to regular passenger trains in 1934). CIE Class B Bo-Bo No B162 and stock will return empty to Tralee to form a second excursion train.** *John Langford*

Left: **This September 1960 picture sees CIE Class J15 0-6-0 No 133 with the lifting train on the Valentia Harbour branch. This line held the distinction of being the most westerly railway in Europe, and from January 1957 motive power had included the new Class C Bo-Bo diesels.** *Colour-Rail*

84

Above: **CIE Class J9 0-6-0 No 249 waits on the causeway approaching Dungarvan with the 1.00pm goods from Waterford in October 1962. Built in 1912, Nos 249-52 were originally allocated Class 249 but were re-designated Class 351 in 1923. Popular on seasonal beet trains on the Rosslare route, No 249 soldiered on until 1963.** *Roy Hobbs*

Below: **CIE Class C Bo-Bo diesel No C209 is seen negotiating the street section of the Cork City Railways in June 1968. This single line was opened in 1912 to connect Albert Quay with the GSWR station at Glanmire Road. Primarily used for freight transfer, this cross-city link survived until 1976.** *J. Edgington*

Above: **CIE Class J15 0-6-0 No 128 shunts Cork Glanmire Road yard in October 1962. In the background is the chimney for the sand-drying hopper for the locomotive depot. No 128 was one of a total of 67 locomotives to be fitted with the 'Z'-type boiler, the last to have this modification being No 196 in 1953.** *Roy Hobbs*

Below: **CIE Class B1a No 801 *Macha* awaits departure from Cork Glanmire Road with the IRRS/SLS/RCTS tour on 5 June 1961 which it worked as far as Mallow. It had languished out of use for some time at Cork and it was doubted that it would ever haul a passenger train again until it was repaired and partially retubed for this working.** *T. B. Owen*

Above: Previously depicted with a sugar beet train on page 74 CIE Class J15 0-6-0 No 109 is portrayed between duties outside Cork Glanmire Road shed in April 1956. Surviving until 1964, No 109 was one of 59 locomotives to be fitted with the 4ft 4in boiler, a programme commenced in 1882, No 109 being treated in 1912. *J. Edgington*

Below: Another picture taken at Cork Glanmire Road shed, this time depicting CIE Class K4 2-6-0 No 369 in June 1955. This locomotive was the sole survivor of this four-strong class built by the GSWR in 1909. Following the success of the Class 355 another four of the type appeared with this class which were basically similar to the earlier 2-6-0s. *Colour-Rail*

Dublin & South Eastern

CIE Class J18 0-6-0 No 591 is depicted crossing the River Liffey in Dublin on Tara Street bridge on 11 May 1957. The train is traversing the former City of Dublin Junction Railway with what is possibly a boat train from Dun Laoghaire to Dublin Amiens Street or Kingsbridge. *T. B. Owen*

The Dublin & South Eastern Railway was built to serve the area to the south-east of Dublin. It was originally incorporated as the Waterford, Wexford, Wicklow & Dublin Railway Company by Act of Parliament in 1846 and embraced the earliest railway in Ireland, the Dublin & Kingstown which had opened in 1834. Its principal main line took another 40 years to complete and ran along the coastal strip between the mountains of Wicklow and Wexford and the Irish Sea. In 1860 it was renamed the Dublin, Wicklow & Wexford Railway Company and on 31 December 1906 it was again renamed as the DSE.

The Kingstown–Dalkey section was originally operated on the atmospheric system, this principle being employed for the uphill journey to Dalkey, the trains returning to Kingstown by gravity. The line was first tested in August 1843 but it did not live up to the directors' expectations. The disastrous potato famine of 1847 drastically reduced passenger numbers together with mass emigration, and serious engineering problems caused the line to be converted to conventional operation.

The railway formed part of the Royal Mail route between London and Dublin via Dun Laoghaire. The DSE had two main stations in Dublin on separate lines : Westland Row (renamed Pearse in 1966) and a terminus at Harcourt Street. Apart from the main line to Wexford there were also branches to Shillelagh and Waterford.

The original line which in many places followed the coastline suffered badly from erosion, costly diversions being necessary in the early part of the 20th century. Irish railway history was always beset with problems from lack of capital to political troubles and attacks on lines. The DSER did not escape from these, although it suffered less than other lines. It was also affected by economic problems after World War 2 and the closures which followed, although it retained substantial commuter traffic in the south of Dublin and connected with the main routes to England from Rosslare to Fishguard and Dun Laoghaire to Holyhead.

When the DSER was formed in 1907 a significant portion of its revenue was earned from commuter traffic between Dublin and Bray which was in the hands of four-coupled tank locomotives. Longer-distance services were operated by a small fleet of 4-4-0s, goods services being in the main worked by 0-6-0s. New locomotives were either purchased from outside manufacturers or built in 'the Factory' (the old DWWR workshops) at Grand Canal Street, Dublin, and were only ever acquired in modest batches. Whilst new locomotives were 'built' at the Factory the term 'assembled' might be a better description. This was a two-storey converted distillery and was far from ideal for locomotive engineering, no crane being available for lifting locomotives, such operations being achieved by the use of hydraulic jacks to lift one end at at time. It was normal practice to 'buy in' such parts as boilers, cylinders and frames from outside suppliers. When taken over by the GSR the shortcomings were quickly recognised and the entire facility was closed down in 1926. At this time 16 members of the DSER fleet were quickly withdrawn by the GSR and a further six were scrapped shortly afterwards.

On the DSER there was no formal system for classifying locomotives, and in several cases the concept of 'class' was loosely interpreted as there was much diversity within small groups of locomotives of the same basic type. This could have been a product of the physical restrictions that existed at the Factory. There was one common feature that existed on most small DSER locomotives, this being known as the 'Grand Canal Street wheeze'. This noise infuriated residents living along the lineside but apparently did not affect locomotive performance.

With the early closure of the Factory, ex-DSER locomotives were repaired at Inchicore; thus such GSWR features as chimneys appeared sooner than on former MGWR types, which were still being repaired at the Broadstone well into the 1930s.

The DSER had considered the introduction of electricity for its commuter services but a completely satisfactory solution took 60 years to materialise in the form of the Dublin Area Rapid Transit overhead electric train services which were integrated with the ex-GNR commuter routes northwards to Howth and later Malahide.

Right: CIE Class C Bo-Bo diesel No C231 waits at Bray with a Dublin train in May 1959. One year later in 1960 10 members of this class were equipped for electrical train-heating. Introduced to replace the ageing '101' class 0-6-0s the Class C diesels were designed as branch-line locomotives, work which was soon to disappear with the forthcoming branch closures. *Colour-Rail*

Below: With the signal cabin in shot DMU No 2619 is seen leaving Killiney station with an evening Dublin–Bray working in May 1959. Unit No 2619 was built by AEC/Park Royal in March 1953 as a driving second open car and remained in service for 30 years before withdrawal in November 1983. *Colour-Rail*

Left: Work-stained CIE Class A Bo-Bo diesel No A55 skirts the River Slaney west of Wexford with an up Rosslare boat train in September 1958. Diesel-electric locomotives on CIE were not fitted with heating boilers, the trains being heated from special vans in which the boilers were carried, one being visible here behind the locomotive. *D. Cross*

Above: **CIE Class J15 0-6-0 No 114 stands at Wexford North station with the 1.15pm mixed Thursday and Saturday-only 'Market Train' to Rosslare Harbour in September 1958. For the 9¾-mile journey this train was allowed 1hr 20min.**

Below: **CIE Class J15 0-6-0 No 116 is seen moving stock at Wexford North station in September 1958. Wexford North, as the station became known in post-Grouping days, was the terminus of DSER territory, and prior to the 1925 amalgamation formed an end-on junction with the line to Rosslare Harbour some 11 chains south of the station.** *D. Cross (both)*

Cork, Bandon & South Coast

Former CBSCR Class B4 4-6-0T No 464 shunts stock for the IRRS/SLS/RCTS trip along the line to Cobh and back on 4 June 1961 — although there were some regrets that the promised six-wheeled coaches had not been forthcoming. Although it was a Sunday evening, a telephone call produced the desired result, and a special train of vintage six-wheel coaches made the round trip to Cobh late in the evening. *Roy Hobbs*

Operating from Cork and serving the towns along the inland and coastal areas of West Cork, the CBSCR had a route length of 93¾ miles, all single track. The railway carried considerable tourist traffic, with many road car routes connecting with the line, including the Prince of Wales Route from Bantry to Killarney as well as heavy fishing traffic from Bantry and Kinsale.

It was incorporated under the Cork & Bandon Railway Act of 1845 and opened for traffic between Bandon and Ballinhassig in December 1851, a service of coaches being maintained pending the completion of the tunnel between the latter place and Cork. The company suffered financial problems for the first 25 years as access to Cork required two major civil engineering works, the Ballinhassig Tunnel and the Chetwynd Viaduct. Also known as Goggins' Hill Tunnel, Ballinhassig Tunnel was a ½ mile in length, its construction delaying overall completion. The Chetwynd Viaduct carried the line over a valley and the main road to Bandon for over 100 years between 1851 and 1961. It was designed by Charles Nixon (a former pupil of Brunel) and constructed between 1849 and 1851 by Fox, Henderson, the same company which built the Crystal Palace in London. Standing 91ft high, it consists of four 110ft spans, each span composed of four cast iron ribs, carried on masonry piers 20ft thick and 30ft wide. Both the tunnel and the viaduct can still be seen and accessed.

The Cork & Kinsale Junction Railway, incorporated in 1859, was worked by the C & B Company at a mileage rate, until purchased in 1879. The West Cork Railway from Bandon to Dunmanway was opened for traffic in June 1866, but worked as an independent company. The Ilen Valley Railway which was opened for traffic on 21 July 1877 extended from Dunmanway to Skibbereen. The Cork & Kinsale line was taken over as from 1 January 1880, with the lease of the Ilen Valley Railway and power to construct the Bantry extension, opened on 1 July 1881.

The Clonakilty Extension, opened in 1886, and the Baltimore Extension, worked by the CBSCR. The Timoleague & Courtmacsherry Railway which opened in December 1890 was more or less self contained, although through summer excursion trains ran in GSR and CIE days.

In 1909 the Ilen Valley Railway was acquired by the Bandon company. The railway was incorporated into the Great Southern Railways (Ireland) in 1924, this being in turn incorporated into Córas Iompair Éireann in 1945. In an effort to reduce costs CIE introduced diesel multiple-units in 1954. Due to economic problems, competition from road traffic and falling passenger numbers the line closed on 1 April 1961. The tracks were later sold to Nigeria and the land of the permanent way to local farmers.

Despite the ¾-mile connection over the Cork City Railways (not opened until 1912) the CBSCR was in the main physically remote from the Great Southern & Western network. Its locomotives had their own distinctive character, and at the amalgamation it operated exclusively tank engines, although early in the company's history some 2-2-2, 2-4-0 and 0-4-2 tender engines had been used. Until 1874 the company had come to rely on second-hand machinery, a policy that proved to be unreliable and expensive.

The 4-6-0T 'Bandon Tanks' were the best known of the company's locomotives and were the only engines of the type to be built by Beyer Peacock. This wheel arrangement gave a cramped rear end and limited coal capacity, but the relatively short distances travelled by these engines did not present problems with their use. In GSR days most of the class continued to work the former CBSCR section, although No 468 was allocated to Grand Canal Street shed in the summer of 1929 and was used on boat trains as well as Dublin–Bray commuter services.

Maintenance of the company's locomotive fleet was quite an achievement in view of the cramped conditions of its workshops at Rocksavage. Close to the throat of the Albert Quay terminus and set at 90° to the running lines, the workshops were in a two-road 290ft building where all repairs were undertaken. The locomotive sidings known as 'The Quarry' were hemmed in on two sides by cliffs and had no covered accommodation. Under the management of the GSR, works activities were restricted to carriage and wagon repair.

Top: **The layout at Cork Albert Quay can be clearly seen in this picture as CIE Class J26 No 560 is busy with shunting duties in October 1962. Just out of view on the left is the single line leading out onto the street section of Cork City Railways, a line which managed to outlive the CBSCR by some 15 years.**

Above: **CIE Class J26 0-6-0T No 560 with two vans is seen coming off Victoria Quay is about to enter the CBSCR Albert Quay yard in October 1962. Often called the 'Irish Terriers' these locomotives resembled the London, Brighton & South Coast Railway Class A1/A1X tanks in looks.**
Roy Hobbs (both)

Right: This charming picture taken at Clonakilty sees CIE Class C Bo-Bo No C210 which has arrived with the 7.00pm from Clonakilty Junction on 24 May 1958. This was the terminus of this branch in County Cork. Behind the branch train of one van and a single bogie coach is the one-road engine shed. *J. Edgington*

Above: Silver-liveried CIE Class C diesel No C232 has arrived at Courtmacsherry with the inaugural through diesel excursion from Cork Albert Quay in May 1958. By this time the main traffic on this branch from Ballinascarthy was the seasonal sugar beet plus the occasional seaside excursion. *J. Edgington*

Right: The CBSCR section of CIE was handed over to diesel traction quite early — the Cork–Bantry passenger trains in 1954 and the regular goods services in 1957. But steam remained on the Timoleague & Courtmacsherry section for the last sugar beet campaign of 1960/1. The locomotive working the beet traffic was stabled overnight by the end of Courtmacsherry station. On Friday 4 November 1960 CIE Class J26 0-6-0T No 552 is ready for another three trips with sugar beet to Ballinascarthy on the Clonakilty branch. *John Langford*

Above: **Former CBSCR Class B4 4-6-0T No 463 is seen a few miles east of Bantry whilst engaged on track recovery of its parent railway in June 1962. By mid-September the line from Bantry was removed as far as Aughaville; the Baltimore line was lifted to Skibbereen, whilst the branch to Courtmacsherry terminated at Skeaf.**

Below: **In the last month of operation, March 1961, CIE Class C Bo-Bo No C220 has arrived at Skibbereen with the 1.55pm from Drimoleague. With the single-road engine shed on the extreme right of this picture, this scene was to be short-lived, the line closing with effect from 1 April.**
Roy Hobbs (both)